How Two
Have a Successful Relationship

How Two

Have a Successful Relationship

By Phil and Maude Mayes

Olive Branch Communications Inc.
Santa Barbara, California, 2016

ISBN 978-1523940110

Printed in the United States of America

Dedicated to spreading peace
one relationship at a time.

Table of Contents

Acknowledgments

Our sincere thanks to all the couples who graciously let us interview them for this book, to our editors, Mitchell Bogatz and Jinjee Talifero, and to our wonderful writers' group for all their support and feedback.

Another Way

WE LIVE a conflict-free relationship. It's been more than a decade now full of peace, love, joy and passion. Friends check in with us every so often: "So you still haven't had any arguments?" The answer is always "No."

It became clear to us very early on that this was a different kind of relating – that we had a way of flowing around obstacles rather than colliding with them. It didn't arise from initial euphoria smoothing the way; instead, something previously unknown to either of us was happening.

The experience is radically different. It is so foreign to the usual view of relationships that you may find it hard to believe. We are two very independent and different people. You may imagine that in order to achieve this peaceful state, we don't speak our true minds to each other, or that at least one of us must always be compromising. Nothing could be further from the truth. We have a very relaxed, open and honest communication and always speak freely without the need for defense. We enjoy and celebrate our differences, and they are never a source of argument. How do we do it? The answer to that question is the very heart of this book. We have examined our behavior and processes and believe that they are available to you as well.

One of the primary things necessary to have this experience is to believe it is possible. An obstacle to this is the belief that conflict is inevitable within a relationship. This myth has become so insidiously inculcated in today's culture that most people take it as a normal part of relating. In fact, many relationship experts extol the virtues of arguing and conflict, and praise all the good that will come of embracing and working through these problems.

"Nonsense!" we say to all of this. Open your minds and your hearts to another way. We are living proof that it is possible to love without hardship and difficulty. You do not always have to struggle and work in order for your relationship to be full of calm, ease, and at the same time, juicy passion.

We are not suggesting that both of you will always see things the same way. Difference and even disagreement are not the same as conflict, argument or estrangement. No couple agrees on everything, but there are ways to resolve issues that, improbable as it may sound, reach a solution that works for both people without requiring any compromise. Such solutions do, however, require that the core values of the two people are aligned. Sometimes there is a tension at the heart that can never be resolved, and this is probably a relationship that should go no further. However, don't take simple differences as an excuse to give up at the first hurdle.

In building a relationship, sometimes we are initially unable to see things in a new way; it's like not being able to find your keys in a room until someone points them out on the table. Once you can accept the possibility that there is another way of relating, you can learn to practice it and share in the joys of a conflict-free relationship.

Another important component to this experience is that once you believe it is possible, and know how to practice this process, you will still need to apply intention. It is your intention toward peaceful relating that will open the door for you and allow you to walk down this path. You can understand the practice, but it takes clear intention to succeed.

We believe that this is something that many couples can achieve, and we are convinced that it can be applied to all kinds of relationships as well. In fact, we are certain that we can change the world in this manner, spreading peace one relationship at a time.

Acceptance

SQUABBLES in a relationship are like stones in your shoes; they don't have to be there. They often come from not fully accepting your partner. Learning about acceptance within a relationship is a way to avoid hobbling along, always being irritated by that stone. People often reject the term "acceptance" because they take it to mean "having to put up with." We have a different approach, and see the acceptability of actions as lying on a spectrum.

How did we come to this? For us, the practice of acceptance came almost unawares. As we got to know each other, we learned how the other acted, behaved and responded in the world. There were none of those discrepancies that can set off alarm bells as you get to know someone: he says he cares about the environment, but leaves trash everywhere without noticing; she describes herself as loving nature, but only watches it on TV.

In our case, we learned that our actions matched our words, and this created trust and a knowledge that we had the same values. It was at first a visceral thing, a bodily sense of comfort, rather than an intellectual understanding; it was only later that we came to speak about it. We had a growing sense of ease, coming to trust each other more and more in everything, and realized we were on the same side, with no need to criticize specific behaviors; we made no judgments, no demands, no attempts to change each other. The more we practiced this, the better we became at it, and more than a decade later, we revel in the experience that this kind of acceptance provides.

The Spectrum of Acceptance

Actions have a wide range of acceptability. Think of actions as lying on a spectrum. At one end are core values, both universal and individual.

Universal core values derive from the relationship between all people – that of being one family – the basic understanding that we are all related, all equal, all brothers and sisters. Also called the Golden Rule, every major religion and philosophy has a version of this.

Individual core values are how each person puts these universal values into practice in their daily lives and their relationships. They will vary according to each person, reflecting, for example, choices of religion, philosophy, politics and relationship to the environment. They come from our background, families, communities, and various other elements of the outside world. As we grow, have our own experiences, and come to know ourselves better, these individual core values will align more and more with universal values.

In the beginning of a relationship, evaluate your new partner in terms of your core values. You may encounter acts that, for you, are truly unacceptable – lying, cheating, withholding – whatever they may be, the deal-breakers vary from person to person.

My great desire is that these personal relationship values rise to the level of what I call life decisions. I refer to life decisions as the most important things that define who you are. With life decisions, the debate is over. These are decisions that are not open for discussion and are not subject to being revisited. Life decisions occur in your heart, and carry a much deeper level of conviction than decisions that you might revisit on a day-to-day basis.
Phil McGraw, *Relationship Rescue*

If you have truly reflected on what your deal breakers are, and find yours do not match your partner's, this is a relationship that will not work, even when offset by sweeteners like sex or money. It's hard in the beginning of a relationship to make this assessment, and it should not be done too precipitously. Allow time to get to know one another, and to experience what the other person's values truly are. At the same time, be careful you are not swept away by the rush of a new relationship, and don't ignore important information about deal breakers. Don't think, either, that you'll be able to fix them by changing the person. Be honest with yourself in this evaluation and if, after careful reflection, you find that your core values do not match, then trust your judgment. Get out.

In the middle of the spectrum are things of importance that have potential resolutions, like whose parents to visit for Christmas, what color to paint the living room or how to deal with the neighbors. Again, these issues vary, and what is a core value for some may be in the middle for others. The more you know what is of real meaning and value to you, the easier it will be to enter into a loving relationship with another. By applying conscious methods of communication, always remembering you and your partner are on the same side and by being committed to peaceful mutual solutions, these middle spectrum issues can, instead of being a source of friction, be transformed into opportunities to experience more intimacy and a renewed sense of love within your relationship.

Sometimes people let the same problem make them miserable for years when they could just say, So what. That's one of my favorite things to say. So what.
Andy Warhol, *The Philosophy of Andy Warhol*

The last part on the spectrum of acceptance, and one where many people get unnecessarily hung up, is with the little things in life – toothpaste tubes, dog hair, underlining in books. A great example of this is in "Love in the Time of Cholera," where the husband and wife argued so bitterly over whether or not there was soap in the bathroom that they stopped talking to each other entirely for four months. So take a careful look at how important these things are to you. What do they represent? If they really are important, then they live in some other part of the acceptance spectrum; if not, there are ways to change how they affect you and to reach decisions about these resolvable issues without conflict.

Acceptance Does Not Mean Compromise

Often when people think about the issue of acceptance, they think it is about compromise. Compromise is the act of giving up something to get something else. It assumes that there are different sides, and that one must settle in order to avoid conflict. It does not allow for the possibility that a resolution can be found, a resolution where, instead of giving up or changing something, you can create a solution that was not originally imaginable to either person. Without putting down compromise or its benefits, we are discussing a different path – one that is not about giving up on some part of yourself, your wants and perhaps even needs, but rather a path that, by acting in union, allows you to find new mutual solutions.

A Conversation

MAUDE: We've often talked about the fact that we don't see acceptance the same as the word compromise. While not really putting down compromise.

PHIL: Yeah, the peculiar thing is that we seem to have found a way to agreement without either of us having to compromise, and it's a very mysterious process because neither of us compromise at all and yet we reach somewhere that works for both of us.

MAUDE: In order for that to happen, the place we reach is different from the place that either of us started at, and there is a feeling of having gotten exactly what we want. There's no feeling of having given something up.

PHIL: Right, right. One of the requirements for that to happen is that I must be open to a series of outcomes; in other words, I am not locked into my initial idea of what I want or how it should be. It's a question of not being attached to that and accepting other possibilities; no, not accepting, but looking at what other possibilities work and looking at why am I attached to my current position and what's the core energy behind it, and how could that be fulfilled in some other way in the world.

MAUDE: It's also important that you know that the other person really wants to hear how you feel – what is important to you – and that they're open to incorporating that into their own experience. Not changing their view to yours, but being open to finding something that incorporates yours and theirs.

PHIL: Yes, and part of that process is active listening. That's the experience of paying attention to the other person and listening to what they say, instead of getting busy with your own thoughts or working out what your response is going to be. Active listening is the experience of really hearing the other person.

MAUDE: And by hearing them, by actually being there, being available to hear, not being busy somewhere else, like in your head, waiting until you can talk yourself or holding onto an idea that you want to say as soon as there's a space – you can be fully there, wanting to hear.

PHIL: I think that when I'm really listening, I hear two things. Firstly, I hear an alternative possibility: oh, we could see this movie instead of that; we could go at 4:30 instead of 7; we could put them to the left of the garden path. Those are trivial examples, but the same idea applies to deeper issues. Whatever is being offered is another possibility for me to look at and think "Hmm, how does that feel compared to this?" And the other thing that I get by really listening to you is to hear where you're at, and to respond to that.

MAUDE: I don't want to put compromise down, but the image that I have of it is that it's not dynamic. Each person is sitting with what they feel they have – this is how it is – and they both want to find some solution that they can be comfortable with, but each of them has already finished observing the issue; they have a finished product. It's like you're in this little box, you've decided this is how it is for you, and any part of change is about compromises, like giving something up to make the other person feel better, or to come to a conclusion, but it's not about having an experience of something new, of creating together.

PHIL: Right, and maybe there's an implicit or explicit belief that the position that you have is the best of all possible positions.

MAUDE: It's frozen, it stays like that, you have your position, there's nothing more to be said in relation to that

that might turn out to be something else entirely.

PHIL: When you think about it, it's actually quite a conceit to think that you have found the very best of all possibilities.

MAUDE: Mmm. Well, you're selling yourself very short by doing that, because you think that nothing can ever get better, or different in a way that's going to add something. You think anything different is going to take something away.

Accept Differences

Instead of thinking in terms of compromise, accept that other people think differently and do things differently, and that small differences aren't a threat to you. They need not be seen as a challenge to your integrity. They are not criticisms of you; they are just instances of the many possibilities in the world.

A common way to deal with such differences is by pointing them out and attempting to influence your partner's behavior, but this is usually unfruitful. It's really important to understand how corrosive criticism is – it's more powerful than you think. The chance of it actually changing someone is pretty slim; it's far more likely to make them defensive and retaliatory. The marriage researcher John Gottman writes that "*as long as there is five times as much positive feeling and interaction between husband and wife as there is negative, we found the marriage was likely to be stable.*" We do not believe that negative interactions have any constructive use. Gottman is saying that if you dilute a poison sufficiently, it won't kill you; that still doesn't mean it's good for you.

Acceptance of the other means letting them do their own thing. If we see them as less skilled or capable than us, the temptation is to chide them or correct them, but these are parental responses. Even offering help can be an implied criticism of their capabilities. Furthermore, our perception of their incompetence may be misplaced; perhaps they just like doing it that way, or maybe they actually do know better than us.

A friend is someone who gives you total freedom to be yourself – and especially to feel, or not feel. Whatever you happen to be feeling at any moment is fine with them. That's what real love amounts to – letting a person be what he really is.
Jim Morrison

All of these reactions are attempts at control, of being attached to a particular outcome. Let things go unless they concern core issues. Someone giving relationship advice once said, "Pick your battles." But why do battle at all? Being "right" does not usually get you where you want to go. When one practices acceptance, there is a noticeable lack of power struggles and an absence of needing "to be right." The more you know yourself, the more you will be able to do this.

If you're in a relationship, take another look at the Spectrum of Acceptance and assess whether or not you and your partner's core values are aligned. Be honest with yourself and realize that there will undoubtedly be issues that fall in the middle of the spectrum that require accepting and open communication to find positive mutual solutions. In the chapter on "Our Process", we offer a way to find these solutions. Other than core values and middle spectrum issues, everything else should be the province of the individual, and not something for you to criticize, try to change or have control over. Instead, rejoice at the very different way that this person is living in the world, yet is still in harmony with your principles.

It is when your partner's behavior disturbs you, but is not in contradiction with your beliefs and life goals, that you need to practice acceptance. What is it that gets under your skin about your partner? What are the annoying little things that you keep stumbling over? Is it your life's goal to live in a world where the dishes always have to be done immediately? Do the napkins have to be folded a particular way? How often should the trash be taken out? Does your partner need to drive the same route to the store that you do? These out of sync episodes can often turn into arguments and real breaches between you and your partner.

A Conversation with Matt

MATT: I think it's really important that both people don't try to be right all the time. I want to share a story about Hayley and me. It concerns one of our biggest arguments. When we were talking about getting married, she told me that she wanted to keep her last name. She said that women shouldn't have to give up their identities to suit their husbands. I understood the merits of the argument from a feminist perspective, but I hated that our household wouldn't be unified under one last name. We both agreed that our hyphenated last name would have sounded horrible! She jokingly said that I should take her last name, to which I said that my friends and family would tease me far too much about that one – that, for good or bad, it was acceptable for a woman to take on her husband's last name, but not the other way around. The arguments got really bad. Neither of us wanted to compromise. It almost ended the relationship. Finally, we found something we could both agree on that, for us, didn't feel like a compromise. Both of our last names shared a single letter – a "Z" – and so we decided that, if we should get married, we would both change our last name to "Z". That would allow for unity in our names and in our childrens' names, which was what I wanted, and it would allow her to hold onto her feminist ideals without feeling like she was giving up her identity. If we had just sat down without judgment in the beginning, without being so sure that our way was the only way, we might have come to that conclusion quite a bit quicker without the drama – but we didn't. We were both so convinced that our way was the only way, it almost cost us the relationship.

Know Yourself

Whatever your differences are, they are worth taking a look at, not so much in relation to your partner, but rather in relation to yourself. Are these things really meaningful to you? If so, what is their meaning to you and do you want them to carry such weight in your life? To avoid these clashes, you must gain a good understanding of yourself. The more you know, the more you can share with another person.

To love oneself is the beginning of a lifelong romance.
Oscar Wilde

Getting to know yourself is an ongoing process, and one that is an integral part of a successful relationship. What is a relationship if not the ability to relate to one another – to understand each other and feel each other's joys, desires, fears and sorrows? In order to share these things, we must know them.

But why wouldn't you know them already? Well, there are a number of reasons why you might be estranged from your own feelings. Firstly, they may too painful to face. It's impossible to say what they might be for you: fear of abandonment, of being trapped, of sex, of criticism. Maybe there are aspects of yourself that you don't like, and don't want others to see: that you're mean, or scared of people, or curse at other drivers. It may be an aspect of yourself that you're fine with, but your social circles aren't: you're an atheist or believe in angels.

You protect all of these internal feelings with a social persona constructed to match the culture you live in. Your parents and society told you and continue to tell you how you should be and act. It is hard to decide how much of this advice is appropriate and how much of it furthers someone else's agenda. Family, friends, television, magazines and employers all issue a constant stream of dictates on how we should live. We act to fit in with the crowd without even realizing it. James Burke demonstrated this on television by arranging for everyone in his audience to stand when he said a certain word. Everyone, that is, except one mark, one victim, who was not in on the secret. As the word was spoken, the camera captured him in slow-motion: astonished, he looked left, then right, then rose along with the rest of the audience without the slightest rational reason for his action.

Given this exquisite dance that we perform with and for each other, it becomes hard to distinguish what we want to do from what others want and expect us to do; it is like trying to hear one's heartbeat during happy hour.

These learned behaviors become what you automatically present to the world, but they are not all that you are; they are not your inner self. Often that's OK. It's not that you should live 24/7 with every raw emotion exposed. Social graces exist for a reason. But the ability to drop them and show your true self to your partner is key to having a fulfilling relationship.

By becoming awake to our transient feelings, and being able to consciously pay attention to them, we can learn to gradually exit the realm of reactive emotional responding, and learn to become more expressive of our immediate emotional feelings and needs.
Jerry Duvinsky, PhD

Finding yourself is not like solving a crossword puzzle, where once it's done, it's done. It is a continuing journey. Pay close attention and find what works for you. Make time away from the distractions of the world. Run, hike, see a therapist, meditate, or whatever it takes for those voices to dissipate and for your true self to show through.

Sometimes when we look inside ourselves at what pushes our buttons, we find that these are old things, things we have outgrown or no longer need to respond to. A good house-cleaning of the old stuff that you are still carrying will often lead to a freer inner self that is more able to live in acceptance with another. How many of your responses are left over from another time or another relationship? Do you still want to hold onto those things for yourself? The less we carry of meaningless reactions from the past, the more we can revel in the joy of the present. Self reflection will strengthen the following skills.

- Being able to step back and look at how you interact with the world, rather than just reflexively acting.
- Separating desire and action—just because you have feelings, doesn't mean you have to act on them.
- Taking responsibility for your actions and your life.
- Having the ability to put yourself in another's shoes, both by empathizing and by identifying with their feelings, thoughts and attitudes.

A Conversation

MAUDE: I think a very important element of accepting differences is knowing yourself. The more you see the experience and the journey as learning and getting to know yourself, the more you'll be open to things happening in the present, rather than what has already happened or how you might project that things should be. If, say, when something starts bothering you, you notice that your partner has a totally different approach to a plan for the day, or an activity you're going to do together, and you may be getting that feeling "Oooh, I've come up against something totally different, what do I do? Do I dig in my heels, do I grit my teeth, do I insist on doing the same thing, rather than something totally different?" That's always a great opportunity to look at yourself and learn something and grow. I say to myself, "Look at this, what's going on here? Hmmmm. I'm getting a little irritated, agitated in some way. I feel I have to push for my position. What is this about? What's going on here? What's making me react this way, what can I learn, is that something I want to have, do I want to react that way?"

You can look at all those immediate responses and learn something about yourself and grow. And so I think a really big thing in a trusting relationship is that you're more and more enabled to do this practice; you know the other person is supporting you in learning about yourself, so you can take the time to really look at things and not have any feeling that you're going to be attacked while you're doing it. There's no fear of something coming at you because your partner is involved in the same way; they want to learn about themselves and grow from the exchange too.

PHIL: Finding that place where you can always hang out and watch what you're doing is difficult, and in the beginning it's easy to fall off the ledge, but the more you do it, the more you know that place is there.

MAUDE: Yes, and it's attractive because it's such a positive experience that it pulls at you, and the more you do it, the more you strengthen your awareness of that pull.

PHIL: Right.

Intention and Attitude

As we come to know and accept ourselves, we can begin to reach true acceptance of another person. This requires a positive act of intention: the intention toward peace and the intention to find harmonious ways of being together. In other words, that must be your desire, your goal, your dream. Intention is like the oars in a boat: much of the time you can go with the current, but at certain points you have to row to make the boat go where you want it to; you can't just let it drift. Relationships can drift similarly, and if you don't intend to have the best one possible, then it won't happen.

This intention towards harmony fosters a basic attitude that is also a critical component of acceptance. We can describe this basic underlying attitude as "positive viewing", or looking with favor upon your partner. We all see what we look for. If your interest is windows, that is what you notice when you look at a building. Think of the glass half-full/half-empty metaphor; if your attitude is one of always observing what is missing, or what should be changed, then that is what your attention will be drawn to. When you focus on what is flawed in your partner, that is what you will see, and you are setting yourself up for disappointment. They'll be too talkative for you one day, and too uncommunicative the next. Nobody will ever be good enough for you. It's impossible!

Your attitude determines where you put your attention; do you see the socks on the floor or the flowers he left for you on the dresser? When you look for positive characteristics, you will tend to see them. Look for and admire your partner's positive qualities, and you will never cease taking pleasure in how wonderful they are.

What happens when you choose to approach your relationship with a spirit of acceptance is that you will automatically find yourself focusing on your partner's assets and qualities rather than on his or her shortcomings.
Phil McGraw, *Relationship Rescue*

This practice is not about making changes in your partner. Instead, you change your own intention and attitude: you want to come together, you want to experience the other person, you want to grow yourself, you have an intention towards peace and goodness. This changes the whole dynamic and creates a safe and loving way of being together.

The 100% Factor

We have a favorite way of describing total acceptance of the other, of who and how they are. We refer to it as the 100% factor. The importance of 100% cannot be underestimated; it is nothing like 99%, because anything less involves measurement, division, in and out, good and bad. The extraordinary freedom to be yourself that comes from this kind of acceptance can only be achieved by 100%. If your partner does not grant you 100% autonomy, there are aspects of yourself that cannot be shared, and to remain a complete person, you must withdraw and separate in order to keep those parts of yourself alive. This process of emotional separation and reconnection has its own cost. The dance and negotiation of acceptance has to be performed anew each time. When there is some small corner within your partner that is still holding back acceptance, you never know when it might rear its head and bite you, so you must still always be guarded to some degree or another. But when each partner is assured of complete acceptance, it is transforming and wonderfully liberating; by being completely ourselves, we are that much more real, authentic and trustworthy to the other.

Imagine you are barefoot on a dance floor. When you know that there is nothing on the floor, no thumbtacks or other dangerous items, you can be free to dance about, flying through the air, unmindful of where you come down. As soon as you introduce a single thumbtack anywhere on the floor, you are no longer able to leap and prance freely. You must always be careful you don't come down on the tack and injure yourself. This very knowledge inhibits you all the time, even if it's just a little bit.

It is the same within relationships. The more thumbtacks that appear in the exchange, the more you must be careful, defended, withdrawn, on alert. Once you reach the threshold of 100%, your mind is not busy with whether the person is right or wrong, or needs changing or adjusting. Instead, when you accept yourself and the other and go forward in the freedom that this way of being brings, it creates an exquisite experience of peace and joy.

This is not to say that people should tolerate anything and everything, acting like a doormat and letting their partner walk all over them. Instead, acceptance is only possible in a partnership that has core agreements in place. As previously mentioned, they vary from couple to couple, but some examples might be trust, honesty, fidelity and fiscal approach. When your values are in agreement, nothing else is necessary. You can give your partner the space to do and be anything.

The 100% factor is not a process. It is a transformation. You either move into 100% or you don't. The effect of this complete openness cannot be emphasized enough. It produces a quantitative change in the experience. We have found that with this underpinning our relationship, there is no limit to the peace, love and joy that we can experience together. This openness feeds on itself, creating an ever-increasing bond. It fills us with strength and security to go about our daily challenges.

Projections and Preconceptions

Lack of projections and demands is critical to acceptance. Many people have their heads filled with everything they think they need to make things work, in any situation and in every relationship. They have so many things decided in advance – what they need in common and how things have to look and feel – that there is very little room for anything to actually just be, never mind allowing something new to come into being.

When you have shared meanings and values as your basis for agreement and union, then you can let go of determining the specifics. You can enjoy the experience of another person, one who is totally unique, and celebrate the fact that they are different. You can be constantly enriched by the other. You will be able to reside in the present, experiencing what is, without preconceptions. If you don't try to fit the other into an idea or a mold or a picture of what could or should be, you can experience what is.

A Conversation

PHIL: I am eternally grateful for the way that you let me be completely myself without any pressure. The result is a very wonderful experience of freedom. It's a remarkably different experience of being myself without having to adjust in any way to your expectations of me. The different quality this brings is hard to believe; it's like the freedom I feel being alone, except that you're here too.

MAUDE: I don't really have any sense that you want me to be different than how I am. As a matter of fact, the feeling that I have is so wonderful because I feel that you see me for who I am, the same way that I see me. You actually see me, and you talk about it and you acknowledge it, and you also appreciate what you see and it gives me a tremendous feeling to know that. At the same time I never feel like you're trying to make me into something, or demand of me to be other than I am, or criticize me for how I am. Instead, I feel tremendous support, surrounded by this very loving feeling, that there's really somebody there who's my partner and who is there with me; we're on the same side, we're not estranged, trying to change each other. You're just never jiggling at the innards of who I am, my own personal self.

PHIL: Yeah, and there's really nothing to get us started. I give you space and you give me space, and that's it; there's nothing that begins to aggravate me. In a way, that sounds silly; there must be, right? But those little potential starting points, we either ignore or simply say, can you close the door when you go out of the room because it leaves a draft, and it's over before it begins, so there's never anything between us to create irritation.

MAUDE: There is always this sense of we, rather than you, you, you, you did this, some accusatory demand or tone. We never get alienated from each other in that way because neither of us does it to the other. We're together, the sense is of being together, and that's why I say we're on the same side. This lack of defense that occurs when you don't feel that you're going to be attacked is really an extraordinary experience in and of itself.

PHIL: Do you think that this experience, once it is grasped, that its very existence is the reason that we remain in balance?

MAUDE: Yes, it's not an intellectual thing, at least not only an intellectual thing, where you're thinking to yourself, "I don't want to get out of sync with this great feeling", or thinking "I don't want to rock the boat." It's not a thought, it's a visceral sensation of togetherness and of peace, of this enormous openness and relaxation – and that's something you would never step outside of by choice.

PHIL: Right. Thoughts are actually slower than emotions; the research shows that the emotion arises and then the thought follows and rationalizes it, so you're right to say that first there is the visceral experience. It's not like we see the dishes and go "Hmmm, I won't say anything about that"; instead there isn't any emotional push away from the center that we are in together.

MAUDE: Yes, and there's a pull into it. It is extraordinarily healthy and attractive.

PHIL: Right, and you've used this term before, that you get a taste for it.

MAUDE: And develop an appetite.

PHIL: Part of our problem of explaining this to people is that if they've never tasted mangoes, how likely are they to say "Oh yeah, I want mangoes in my life"?

Acceptance, Appreciation, Acknowledgment

We all yearn to be accepted and seen for who we really are. We all feel best when recognized as our true selves. You will find that the more you are actually familiar with who you are, the more you appreciate others recognizing that in you as well.

In any relationship, the strongest glue that brings union between people are the three A's: to be accepted for who we are, to be appreciated for who we are, and to be acknowledged for who we are.

To be fully seen by somebody, then, and be loved anyhow – this is a human offering that can border on miraculous.
Elizabeth Gilbert, *Committed: A Skeptic Makes Peace with Marriage*

This chapter has been about the importance of acceptance, but that is not enough by itself. Appreciation is important as well. It goes beyond acceptance; it is a positive feeling about the other, a positive pleasure in aspects of the other person.

And yet, if you never communicate that, the other person has no idea; your good feelings stay locked within you. Just because you see it doesn't mean that your partner telepathically knows it. When you acknowledge the good things in your partner, they feel seen and appreciated. Say it in words and show it in actions.

In a relationship where you feel you have to defend yourself, you cannot afford to be openly vulnerable, and you will not share all of who you are. Appreciation and acknowledgment only feel genuine in the context of full acceptance. When that is not present, even when receiving praise and thanks from your partner, you know that it isn't really you they are seeing. Only when you feel fully seen do the appreciation and acknowledgment feel genuine. When that is the case, it leads to an experience of deep intimacy which makes the "we" of a relationship a living reality.

The Golden Rule

Just as this is true for ourselves, it is true for others as well. When we can place ourselves in our partner's position, even imperfectly, and see that, like us, they want to be accepted, appreciated and acknowledged, then we have the opportunity to act in those ways. And when we do, that liberates them and allows them to be free and share their inner selves with us.

When we acknowledge our partner with all their individuality, and celebrate the differences, we bring about a climate of peace and support within our relationship. When our partner rejoices in getting to truly know us as a unique individual, we become more than we were previously. By living in such a state, we can inspire, influence and teach others, and our relationship becomes a vehicle for peace on earth.

Conversations with Other Couples

DIANE AND MARK

Q: Tell us about acceptance.

DIANE: I would have to put mutual respect at the top. I have a great respect for who Mark is as a person, and for his integrity. I don't think he would ever do anything to harm me in any kind of intentional way. When we have conflict, I may in the moment take it personally, but I feel like this is a person I respect, so I have to give credence to his point of view, though sometimes not always in the moment.

Then there's having good will toward each other that we've built up over time, and that comes from feeling like you can be honest with the other person and that they may not always like what you say but that there's a willingness to listen. I have learned at my age that I don't want to be stuck in a place of yuckiness, of feeling bad, so I'm more willing to overlook something or even see the other point of view or drop something. I don't want to stay in anger or a resentful place or a blame place, because we do a lot better when we're not in that place.

Q: Do you have basic core values you share?

DIANE: Two things come to mind: a sense of humor about life in general and a lot of mutual things that we do together that we enjoy. There's a lot of mutuality in our ideas about the world, enjoyment of how we choose to spend leisure time and that we have similar interests —

that's a big factor – and an appreciation and aesthetic sense that's very similar. Also, in terms of our day to day living, we live very much in the same way: we're both not sloppy people, we both like neatness, we like to have order, we've worked out routines with each other to give each other space.

MARK: Politically, we're both aligned.

DIANE: Political alliance is huge for me.

MARK: We both have very similar aesthetics we talk about.

DIANE: One core value is family. I think we both share a sense that our families are very important to us, so that to me is a big core value. We also have similar goals in terms of wanting to have a certain level of comfort in our lives. How the person is with money – that's a huge issue.

MARK: Also we have made a decision that we're for each other, and even though she has a lot of male friends, I never doubt her fidelity. She never feels that I have a roving eye, so I think that's a core value that we've really worked on, and I try not to even give the impression that there is any reason to be jealous or to use that as a ploy or something like that.

DIANE: That's a trust issue too; we trust each other. I don't think Mark would do anything to intentionally hurt me – and I think Mark knows no matter what I may have said that my intent is not to hurt him.

JAMES AND RITA

Q: Tell us about acceptance.

JAMES: The answer to us is friendship. We just like and

respect each other. And we're both kind and generous people, and so we take care of one another.

RITA: I think we're both givers. I've never dated a giver. It's like we give to each other, we support each other and we don't control each other; we let each other be free, but I don't mean we have an open relationship, because fidelity is important to us.

Q: Do you have basic core values you share?

RITA: I think we like each other. My goal was to actually meet somebody that I liked. So that was the most important thing, because people fall in love, and then reality sets in and they don't like each other. I really like James.

JAMES: Before I met Rita, I was dating, and it just got so frustrating because you meet somebody and put up a front to be more attractive, but then ultimately you have to be honest, so I just decided that I'd had enough. I wasn't going to care about anything any more, and just live my life. So when I would meet somebody, I would just be completely honest and open right on the very first date, and tell her everything about me. All the stuff I'd done right, all the stuff I'd done wrong – just no secrets! And then, if you still want to meet for another date or something that's great, but I'm not going to put up a front.

Q: So, honesty?

JAMES: Yeah, honesty.

RITA: And loyalty.

JAMES: It really worked for us. You know what you're getting right off the bat; I don't think that happens a lot in relationships.

RITA: When I was younger, I had very different priorities, and this time when I was looking for a partner, I wanted somebody I really liked, who was incredibly affectionate, whose touch I really liked, and someone I was attracted to. So it was all touch-based and liking, and I had never had those priorities before. Oh, and no drama. I just wanted something that was easy, whereas before I may have wanted excitement or whatever.

JACKY AND MICHAEL

Q: Do you have basic core values you share?

JACKY: Yeah, total transparency and honesty, and speaking your truth, and sharing with the other person how you want it — not making assumptions that the other person can read your mind. I want to be informed of what he likes, the same way I would like to tell him what I like. It's not fair for him to be guessing and for me to be begrudging something for lack of communication. So communication is a crucial core value.

MICHAEL: It's key. As Jacky said, authentic communication, vulnerable communication, a willingness to hear what might be uncomfortable and might feel threatening to my ego, but I'd much rather hear it now than pretend I didn't hear it or pretend it's not there. And so that is definitely absolute. That and the insistence on being fully present for each other. That, I would say, is also core, a core part of our relationship.

Individuality

Love is union with somebody, or something, outside one-self, under the condition of retaining the separateness and integrity of one's own self.
Erich Fromm, *The Sane Society*

ONE OF THE KEYS to a peaceful and joyous way of relating is to accept and respect each other as two separate and absolutely unique individuals. In our relationship, this is a critical part of how we are with each other. We are both people with a strong and distinct sense of self, and bridle at any attempt to change or control us or to direct what we say or do.

We recognize that what is true personally is also the case for our partner, and therefore we are strongly motivated to honor their individuality and give them the same respect and freedom that we want for ourselves. This kind of separateness does not lead to a lack of connection; on the contrary, it brings us closer, and creates a most joyous environment of undefended openness, trust and intimacy. We share our deepest inner places and at the same time remain independent and separate. As we mesh more and more, we continue to be present as two whole individuals, even as we deepen in our union.

A Conversation

MAUDE: Our time together is so filled with a sense of calm and peace. We don't seem to spend any time on power struggles or on one of us trying to be "right." I never feel I have to defend myself against anything coming from you and so I can therefore be free to fully share myself. In fact, I feel both honored and appreciated for who I am. As time goes on, and we continue to have more and more of the experience of struggle-free relating, we build a trust that this is how it is and will remain for us. What a miracle, and it seems so easy. We just let go and let it be.

PHIL: For me, it starts with non-interference — the position of allowing you to act as you choose, without my attempting to influence your decisions, big or small, as you travel through life.

I do this because I do not want to control you. Why would I take on the burden of that responsibility?

I do this because you are not a child who must be taught the ways of the world for your own good.

I do this because of the pleasure of experiencing

your views, pleasures and desires. Why would I want to narrow my world by making those more like my own?

I do this because I do not feel threatened by you, physically, financially, emotionally. I started with an assumption of trust, and the more time passes the more I am confirmed in this. Another way to put this is that you are practicing the same non-interference.

How cool that you do this too! I am not assailed by criticisms or put-downs; I feel accepted, seen, honored. Because of this, I am able to express myself, be myself, live my life without feeling in any way diminished. On the contrary, I am enhanced by the communication between us that flows so effortlessly because your complete acceptance means there is nothing to inhibit its passage.

Two People

One of the areas that can trip people up is understanding that there really are two separate personalities involved in a relationship. This sounds obvious, but in practice the mind does not always acknowledge this fact. As you grow more intimate with someone, there is a blurring of the line between "you" and "them." You feel the mutual self and sometimes forget there really are two selves, as well as the new self – the couple in union. This type of feeling can quickly lead one down a path of criticism. It creates the desire to alter how or what the other person does, and to try to adjust them to be more correctly representative of one's self.

An example of not recognizing that you are two separate individuals is illustrated by this scene: Bob and Cathy are out with friends. He is telling a story about an event that he and Cathy experienced together. She gets very upset because he is not describing it as she would. This is not the same as Cathy wanting to tell the story from her viewpoint; instead, she wants to cut in and correct his mistakes. Cathy feels as though her story is coming out wrong because she hears what Bob is saying as though it is her voice. She has lost the sense of their separate identities.

What your partner says and does belongs to him or her; you are not responsible for their behavior. Just be with them without trying to control the exchange or the outcome. When you do that, you are less likely to see the other's actions as reflecting on you. For example, don't worry what your friend Jane will think about your partner's bad table manners. That's between them, and truly doesn't involve you. When you're not confusing your partner's identity with yours, you can relax and listen when they bring up something new or different that you would not say or think of in the same way.

These can be tricky areas for a couple to navigate. To remain clear about your separate identities, practice being in the present with each other; when you do, you will experience what is actually there, rather than something you have created in your mind. It is important to empty your mind of preconceptions and expectations. You are then more apt to experience your partner as they are, and not as you would have them be. You are less likely to think they are an extension of yourself, and that therefore they should do what you do or act as you would act.

Being Your True Self

When your partner accepts, acknowledges and appreciates your individuality, it affords you the possibility of attaining true freedom of expression. In order for this to manifest, you have to recognize the opportunities created, and then act on them.

It's easy to act according to your existing patterns, and react based on what you perceive your partner's needs are: do they expect roses; will they be offended at hearing something you might say? Most people are accustomed to subconsciously acting to fit in. It can sometimes be hard to get past the expectations of others and find your own feelings and needs.

As you learn to take advantage of the freedom your partner is offering, you will come to appreciate what a wonderful opportunity this provides for you to be yourself, not someone else's expectations of you. Once you can see this, act on it. Offer your true self: what you want, what you believe, what you feel.

The Paradox of Separateness and Intimacy

When you can relax in your relationship and realize the other person is separate from you, something quite extraordinary and freeing occurs. In the very act of knowing and acknowledging your separateness, you open the door to union. These experiences of separateness and intimacy are seemingly paradoxical.

When you are treated as a different and separate individual, that gives you several freedoms. One is to act independently of your partner according to your own desires. It might be something like seeing your favorite local group at a bar, playing golf with your buddies or going to jazzercise; whatever it is for you, it is something that brings you joy, and yet your partner does not share your interest. When your partner can see you as a different person, understand that you have different satisfactions and interests, and give you the freedom to enjoy them, then you can venture off without feeling guilty.

Another freedom that occurs when you are fully accepted by your partner is that when you are together, you can offer your thoughts and feelings without reserve. You can reveal yourself to another; you can fully express yourself. What an act of intimacy! What a gift! Such acts of vulnerability and sharing are the gateway to closeness and union.

Once the realization is accepted that even between the closest human beings infinite distances continue, a wonderful living side by side can grow, if they succeed in loving the distance between them which makes it possible for each to see the other whole against the sky.
Rainer Maria Rilke

It is the acceptance of each other as individuals that permits both this intimacy and the freedom of autonomy. While it may be a paradox that two such different states arise from this act of acceptance, this blending of separateness and union expands your world – the mental space you live in. How contradictory to logic, and yet so true – being able to fully experience separateness leads to a deeper experience of togetherness.

A Conversation

PHIL: It's almost eerie, the way you let me be myself, in contrast to other people who have always had standards of some sort for me to live up to: standards of tidiness, speech, behavior. I don't feel that from you. I do feel that you have certain expectations as far as sexual loyalty and fiscal responsibility and things like that, but your expectations are so much the way I live anyway, that they are no weight at all.

MAUDE: For me, the strong feelings that I've had from the very beginning have been this very enormous sense of relief. They are comparative feelings, feelings of an absence of things that I've experienced in the past that have been very challenging and stifling, causing estrangement and drama, and it's this sense of relief of you not trying to make me do something or be something that has nothing to do with who I am; of not being asked by you – I don't mean just in words but in expectation levels, in demands, to act a certain way, say certain things, behave in certain ways. Instead, I have experienced this amazing feeling of being known, that you see me for who I am, that you acknowledge me for who I am, and then there is this most wonderful part – that you love me for who I am. You appreciate who I am, and the things that you communicate to me about how you see me or what you love about me are the things that I truly see as me. Those are the things that I, too, value about myself.

PHIL: Well, that might be in part because you show up; you don't hide yourself. That's one of the wonderful things about you, that what you see is what you get — or what I see is what I get, let's put it that way.

MAUDE: And I know, going in the other direction, I have been telling you something about my experience of you, or what I see or so appreciate about you, and you've said "No one's ever said that before, but yes, now that you say it, I can see that it is that way." It's almost like parts of you — I don't know if they weren't shared, or they just weren't seen, acknowledged and appreciated. You seem so surprised that somebody is saying it that way, and then at the same time it's something that feels right and is familiar to you. I think it's because you have also felt so free to be who you are as a result of this lack of manipulation.

PHIL: Yes, and there is a feedback loop here in that not being criticized allows me to be who I am, and the more I don't feel under attack, the more I can show who I am and then the more I can be seen for who I am.

MAUDE: And share even more of yourself.

PHIL: You used a very interesting word earlier on: "comparative". You were comparing how I am with how other relationships have been for you, and that is the same for me as well. In relationships in general, expectations arise as the relationship progresses — but with you, this never occurred.

MAUDE: Yes, for me there is a sense of relief as I kind of breathe and can start not to be on my guard, and let down any walls or stop looking over my shoulder, or thinking "Is the ball going to fall on my shoulder, on my head? Is someone is going to come in and demand of me to be something entirely different than I am, or say it different, or want something different?" All that has been completely absent with us.

PHIL: Yes. The question is, how did we come to this?

MAUDE: By a lot of work on our individual selves that has probably brought each of us into a place of being present, not like being filled up with what you want or how it should be, but being willing to step out into the unknown, what is, with a person.

Celebrate the Difference

As you practice this, you will find that you come to appreciate your differences, learning and growing from them, rather than feeling challenged or attacked by these differences. Do you want this person you are with to be a distinct and different individual, or are you looking for agreement and verification of yourself in them? Are you challenged or stimulated by a different approach to the same goal?

There is security in familiarity. The unknown is potentially dangerous, and caution served us well when we were hunters on the savannah. Modern society has tamed most of those threats, but when your partner does something unfamiliar, whether it be minor, like putting the cutlery in the rack the other way up, or something larger for you, it can trigger a sense of unease, and sometimes even a feeling of being threatened. You can't fight feelings like this with intellectual thoughts, so instead focus on the part of you that is drawn to novelty, newness, difference and freshness.

This is your opportunity to celebrate the difference. Stop. Listen. Observe. This is your lover, your partner who you trust, honor and appreciate. They are not you, they are different. They are an entirely unique personality. They add to your world, and bring new colors and new notes. You are in a relationship, not sitting in front of a mirror. Rejoice!

With every human being we meet, we are guaranteed to meet sameness to ourselves and differentness from ourselves as a matter of human fact.... Limiting ourselves to valuing sameness only greatly reduces our possibilities for growth and increases the potential for boredom and destruction.

Virginia Satir, *Making Contact*

It is a wonderful feeling to be accepted for who you are and not have to feel that you are constantly guarding or protecting your being. When your partner shows, by their words and deeds, that they recognize who you are and celebrate who you are, it creates a deep sense of abiding peace, which is strongly empowering. And when you do the same for your partner, the combined effect is transformational.

Conversations with Other Couples

DIANE AND MARK

Q: How do you view the differences between each of you, and how does that affect the relationship?

MARK: That's something we're working on. We know the differences are there, but sometimes it's just so blatant.

DIANE: There are differences in emotional temperature. Mark is much calmer, generally speaking. Contained.

MARK: And more reflective.

DIANE: And I am more outgoing, I mean extroversion vs. introversion. Also I have more energy in a certain way; I can be going, going, going and wanting to do more than Mark, and he needs more time to pull back and do his yoga and reflect. When we travel, that comes into play because we have to negotiate all the time how we're going to spend the day, and when and if we're going to take breaks.

MARK: I don't think that you can change a person – the way they perceive things and how they react. I think you just have to be accepting, so I work more on just accepting the differences. There's a lot of things that you do that I can't even comprehend doing, but I'm glad that you do them.

DIANE: Sometimes differences can be challenging for me. Something happens, and I think, "If it were me I might be doing it a different way," and then it gets into "Is my way the better way?" That puts me into more of a parental way of thinking about you than I like to think about you, and so I have to really guard myself as far as that goes.

MARK: Yeah, and I'm very sensitive to that.

DIANE: And then you get your back up, you know, and sometimes that becomes a cycle.

MARK: So we're really working on that.

ANNE AND JOHN

Q: How do you view the differences between each of you, and how does that affect the relationship?

ANNE: My experience of you is that you are very much in your head, because I think that of the four Jungian aspects of thinking, feeling, sensing and intuiting, that you're very heavy in the thinking quadrant. Of course, you have some of all – we all do – but we do usually favor one of the quadrants, and perhaps we're working on doing a better job of balancing these modes of being. And then there's another quality added on to thinking, feeling, sensing and intuiting, and that is judging or perceiving. I would say you're probably more the introverted, thinking, judging type. Your judging is not a bad thing, but it is an intellectual type. So I think when you're in a situation, what I observe when you interact with people – this includes me – you're more assessing and analyzing. Now, that's not my primary style, I'm more the intuitive, feeling, perceptive type.

JOHN: Mm hmm. Yep.

ANNE: So we have very different personality styles, is what it comes down to. It's a personality strength, and I think that what we learn is that every strength also has weaknesses. And we work on these traits in order to balance them and become aware of them, so we can move along. You're not any one thing because I see you as more on a spectrum, a continuum, and you move along that, and the same for me, but I would be the perceiving and intuitive type which lends itself much more to being present.

Q: How do you deal with both of you being separate individuals and yet still having space within the relationship?

ANNE: I'd like to go back to our marriage vows that we formulated over 18 years ago. They were very much about supporting each other in becoming all that we can be, and I asked you, John, for support in my spiritual practice, and I think you have done your best to support me in that, and I don't think it has always been easy. A lot of my time does go toward other things related to those spiritual goals, and to other people. I think that would be hard for most people to live with. I don't think I'm the main event in your life either; there's a lot of important things in your life, there's a lot of important things in my life, yet we love each other and we value each other, and it's that thing that Rilke said about being the guardians at this vast immenseness that is the other person. That remains mysterious always, and definitely I'm aware of that as the context or situation of our marriage; that we have made this vow to stand guard at the immensity of the other person, and allow that person to become all they can be, knowing we will never know everything there is to know about that other person. We may not even understand all of the things that are driving and motivating that person or their underlying values, which we keep discovering. So I think that we, for the most part, give each other the time and space to follow these personal creative and spiritual goals that each of us have. That's my experience.

JOHN: Mine too. Recently, we've been dealing with some changes in our basic routine. We had a pattern, a rhythm, that when you retired last April, totally changed. All of a sudden you were here all the time, so it changed how we ate, for example. For me it was an adaptation, because when I was in the house, I was pretty much by myself, just me and the cats, and now I'm not, I'm in the house with somebody else, all the time.

And that was quite different. And so for me I found myself struggling to get comfortable and to adapt to that process. You know, knowing who I am and knowing about my own quirks, that I'm a recovering control freak. All of a sudden, you were around all the time, and there were a lot more opportunities for me to control you (laughing). Which of course never worked.

ANNE: I was just going to ask, (laughing) how did that work for you? (Both laugh heartily.)

JOHN: Yeah, that wasn't working too well, and it was kind of frustrating to say the least. All of a sudden I was with you more intensely than ever in our lives together in the last 18 years. For me, it comes down to being as sensitive as possible to your being in the same space.

JAMES AND RITA

Q: How do you view the differences between each of you, and how does that affect the relationship?

JAMES: We're actually really different. I'm not a gregarious person. I'm quiet. So I don't really pursue friendships or going out to parties. And Rita is one hundred percent gregarious. But we get along because if I don't want to go to a party, I don't have to, but it makes her really happy if I do go, so I try to go. As far as parties and friendships and being around people, we're just totally different that way. I'm very predictable; if there's a big crowd over there, then I'm over here, and Rita will be in the middle of the crowd.

RITA: Yes. But I think we've both grown to be more like each other. I'm fast and James is slow and steady, but I've cut down on some of my extra activities, and James has gotten more social since the beginning, so it has calmed me down to be with James. We kind of play off each other. It's been great.

JAMES: To me, it's sometimes a way to improve myself — like if she wants to go to a party, I'll grumble to myself about going, but then I think "Well, wait a minute. You're not really very good with people; it would probably be good if you went to a party and put yourself in that environment." So I convince myself that by doing this, it would actually be a good thing for me, and I change my mind, go to the party, and try to participate and improve myself.

I kind of do that a lot. For example, Rita wants me to help with something or do something, and I initially feel a little resentment because I have all this other stuff to do. But then I wonder if it's really that important, or am I just unorganized, and I see that if I was better organized, I could get done what I want to do and also take part in what she wants me to do, which is going to be fun because it's always fun. And so I try to improve myself just to keep up with Rita, who's really not asking anything out of the ordinary and just wants to have a good time. It's just that I'm such a troll sometimes, and she has to drag me out to events. So it helps me to devote more time to try to be more efficient working, so I have more time to spend with Rita.

Q: How about space in the relationship?

JAMES: Yes, I think that's important; you have to give the other person their freedom. I know people who tried to control their relationship all the time and it ultimately ended because the other person didn't want to be boxed in, and so I think if you really want someone to stay, you have to give them as much space as they want. You just have to give people freedom. I think that's the thing that will make people stay.

Q: You two maintain separate spaces, don't you?

JAMES: Yes, we do. We haven't moved in together; we maintain two different houses, and I think that's been great. I'll be over about five nights a week on the average, but I've got two nights a week at home where I've got my stuff and my mess, and she's got her thing over here the way she wants it, so we're not arguing or fighting over space. It's worked out really well for us.

RITA: We've talked about moving in and we've thought about it, but I'm scared to do that because this is the best I've ever had and I don't want to ruin it. We haven't had a fight in eight years, so I think the arrangement that we have is really nice. Sometimes I long to have more time with James, and that's maybe my biggest longing, but on the other hand I appreciate the romance that comes with seeing the partner at the end of the day and just welcoming him and having that be a special time, rather than being together all day, every day, because both of us have jobs where we don't have a 9-5, so we would be in each other's space all the time. That would be a different lifestyle for both of us, and we might run into some problems, so I haven't been willing to give up the romance for more time together.

JACKY AND MICHAEL

Q: How do you view the differences between each of you, and how does that affect the relationship?

JACKY: He's much more sensitive. He would cry much more easily; I cried one time in three years but he has no problem, no hesitation. I don't seem to be as sensitive as he is, so that makes us different. I'll be strong, I'm independent, and I think he likes that – the fact that I'm independent and strong. We complement each other. I like his sensitivity. What do you think?

MICHAEL: Yeah, that's very accurate. I tend to be, for lack of a better word, more goofy and light-hearted that way, and she is my best audience. I play to an audience and when I see her laugh genuinely to the point where she's almost in tears and doubled over almost in pain, it gives me pure joy to see that. I have a tendency to be a little more optimistic and enthusiastic, where you tend to be pragmatic. But I can also easily think "Oh, that won't work."

JACKY: Sometimes he would say "Oh, that's not gonna work out," and I tend to see the other way around "No, why don't you try that way? Why don't you see this or why don't you say...." I always see some other angle that he doesn't look at; instead of giving up on it, I'm giving him some other ways to do the same thing and perhaps achieve what he's aiming for.

MICHAEL: Yeah, and I really admire that in her.

JACKY: I look and I see things out of the box. Even if it's an unsolved problem, I still go for it. Actually, it's a good thing that we have differences. I mean it would be so boring if we coincided on everything – God no. I celebrate the difference.

Q: How about space in the relationship? You two maintain separate spaces, don't you?

MICHAEL: Well, I think its very easy to fall into a routine and take things for granted.

JACKY: Yes, I think to keep it always fresh, it's important that the man and woman have their own space, and have their work, their responsibilities; and then when they get together, the time is dedicated to being there exclusively for each other. We don't live together right now, although we plan to. I work at home, he works at home, which would make it even more difficult; when you see each other all the time, for me it would be asphyxiating. I need my space, I need to go away, I don't need to see him all the time, believe me, I have plenty of things to do on my own and I love my own company, I don't need him. I'm not a needy person. That's one thing that people should try to avoid, the neediness of that other person. Because that's no good. And it's not healthy. I don't need him to feel good about me, and our relationship.

Our Process

WHEN THERE IS SOMETHING we need to agree on, whether it be a decision we have to make or a problem that needs to be resolved, we have found a way of dealing with it that does not involve any struggle or conflict.

Our approach is simple but very effective. We start by speaking in turn, offering our thoughts and feelings about the situation. Each of us listens and tries to understand the other, rather than defensively preparing counter-arguments.

A willingness to change and a belief that other positions are possible are both critical to this process. Our intention is to be together and to reach a solution or decision that is mutual. We are both fully present with each other, and neither of us has a predetermined answer. By hearing each other and being open, new ideas arise, and for each of us, our landscape of possibilities expands until we meet at a solution that neither of us imagined at the start. A new creation has emerged; something that is the product of both of us together, rather than from just one of us alone.

Neither of us has compromised because the reality is that many outcomes can fulfill our needs, and our original position was just one of them. No one has given anything up; rather, we have both gained something new from the process itself.

This experience is wonderful. The more we practice it, the more we understand how it works, and the more we embrace it. Instead of tension and conflict, it engenders intimacy and closeness, and a great feeling of joy and peace arises which makes us want to experience this again and again. We have moved into a way of accessing our mutual self and finding answers there. Only a solution that is shared can provide this kind of peace and joy.

Is Conflict Inevitable?

All of us have heard over and over that conflict is inevitable within a relationship. The common view is that we must deal with this conflict and learn to work through it. We believe that the essence of this myth is false. Although well-meaning, it perpetuates the view that the partners are adversaries and on different sides, and this attitude often leads to unnecessary separateness and estrangement between couples. It reinforces differences such as gender and personality, and instead of making them something potentially positive, presents them as obstacles to be overcome. Many therapists believe in conflict, and even seem to revel in it:

You and your partner are programmed for conflict. The fact that you are involved with a member of the opposite sex – and I emphasize the word "opposite" – means that you are trying to mesh your life with someone who is physically, mentally, emotionally, and socially different than you. You and your partner are as naturally compatible as cats and dogs, and take my word for it: there is no book, no speaker, and no therapist who can erase that natural difference.

Phil McGraw, *Relationship Rescue*

As much as we like some of Phil McGraw's positions, we categorically reject this view. Instead, we see differences as something to celebrate, and rather than leading to an inevitable conflict, they can be a strength which helps a couple thrive.

A Conversation

MAUDE: It's really interesting how this very basic experience that we have had, of not having conflict and argument, has turned out to be such a radically different experience than most people have. It seems so easy, so simple and so obvious in our experience.

PHIL: Yes, it was actually the first thing that caught our attention if you think about it. We didn't have conflict, so we said "Whoa, what is going on here?" That was the genesis of this entire writing, and I still think it's one of the most important things to explain to people. One of the reasons it's hard is that it is so contrary to the usual expectations.

MAUDE: Yes, and of course we're not saying there is no such thing as a disagreement, like having different approaches or opinions; it's just that we don't have the experience of anger, fighting or needing to be right.

PHIL: The flavor is entirely different.

MAUDE: And there's nothing that's going to cause us to feel estranged from each other or distanced or separated as opposed to in union. I don't mean we're always in total agreement either, I just mean the sense of being together isn't broken or disturbed.

PHIL: Right. One of the consequences of that is that there is no aversion to anything that we need to talk about.

MAUDE: I don't really like drama, I don't seek drama from inside my own person, and in previous relationships, there was quite a lot of drama and arguing, the kind of arguing where you really become estranged from your partner, where there's this gap in the union, this break; not just disagreeing about something, but really fighting, arguing, having conflict, all things that we don't experience. And that has been one of the fabulous experiences with you from the very beginning, we haven't fought, and we haven't had any of that kind of conflict.

PHIL: I think I don't bring it because I don't feel attacked.

MAUDE: So you think a lot of the time people are just feeling attacked and then they fight back? Or somebody just loves drama and wants to be right about everything and wants to control or wants to emphasize their viewpoint.

PHIL: Yeah, I think the control issue is a starting point for lots of friction.

MAUDE: And drama too; many people have been raised to associate drama, arguing and heavy emotions with having feelings and caring. It's maybe what they saw when they grew up. We don't have that, we don't do that. We are very passionate without arguing.

PHIL: Maybe people enjoy the adrenaline, in the same way that people go to Six Flags and enjoy the adrenaline from the roller coaster. If there's no roller coaster, you can get the same effect by tweaking your partner until they react.

MAUDE: Well whatever those things are, they are totally absent in us. We don't seek it, and we don't do it. We have a whole different way of talking with each other.

Take a New Approach

How do you and your partner handle decision-making and problem-solving? There is a simple and surprisingly powerful way of approaching this that can transform your interactions. For most couples, these activities are often a source of tension and conflict, rather than an opportunity for a creative experience together. These sessions frequently feel like duels over who is right, and produce little in the way of mutual satisfaction or inspired solutions.

Instead of tensions and feelings of separation, our process offers a wonderful experience of joint action. It is simple and effective, and can be used by anyone, with often astounding results. Try it out, and with a little practice, you will be surprised at the difference in outcome.

Set the Scene

When conflict is our normal response, it can be difficult to adopt a new approach, but you can change the pattern by making a different and conscious choice. Next time you and your partner have decisions to make or a problem to solve, think of it as a new kind of experience together, and treat it like a shared adventure. Set the scene by making sure both of you are comfortable, relaxed, and will not be hurried or interrupted. It's important that there be no time constraints, and that you can give each other your full attention. Start out by holding hands or being in physical contact, and proclaim to each other that you are on the same side and are looking for a place of mutual agreement. Relax, empty your minds of everything and prepare to enjoy yourselves!

Speak Personally

Everyone has read and heard about how important communication is. But what kind should you use? It is critical to communicate about yourself by expressing your wants and needs. This will add a very important component to your exchanges. Your partner will gain intimate information about you; after all, they can't read your mind. Verbalizing your wants and needs will also put you more in touch with them, because until you can identify and name your feelings, they control you without your assent. Once you name them, you gain more insight into yourself, making it all the easier to share.

Communication is to relationship what breathing is to maintaining life.
Virginia Satir, *Making Contact*

State the issue or problem you are considering. Fully share what you want and what you feel, speaking one at a time until you are done. Avoid using the word "you" (the finger-pointing you); instead, speak personally. Say "I'm cold," rather than "You pulled the blanket off me." Here you are saying how you feel, and not what the other person did. By phrasing it this way, two things are different. Firstly, it is no longer an accusation of the other person's behavior, so it does not provoke a defensive response ("No I didn't!") or a counter-attack ("Well, you did that last night.") It is merely a statement of how the world is for you. Secondly, a statement in the first person is an act of intimacy, a revealing of your self. By speaking about your own feelings, you offer closeness and invite empathy.

Statements which begin "You never" or "You always" are usually ones that generate far more heat than they do illumination. The actual difficulties cannot be clarified when they are being buried under a slag heap of wide-ranging, irrelevant denunciations.
Maggie Scarf, *Intimate Partners*

Hear Your Partner

After you speak from the "I" about your feelings and wants, listen to your partner doing the same, without interrupting or doing any editing in your mind. Actually listen, rather than waiting for the moment when you can talk again about why your opinion is the correct one. It's really important that you do not criticize your partner's suggestions, but simply accept them as their reality. When responding, avoid starting with the word "but", as this gives your partner a sense that you're rejecting what they said. Instead, by simply saying "and", you add to the available possibilities.

Expressing one's own feelings, but being incapable of listening, is a dysfunctional way of being in a fight.
Maggie Scarf, *Intimate Partners*

As this process unfolds, the situation will change for both of you. Each of you now knows what your partner feels and wants. You have more information. Keep sharing, and you will find that other possibilities arise that you did not see before. This is how a mutual solution begins to emerge. Trust that such a place can always be found. When you share core values, this is always possible.

Explore Together

Take your time when having this discussion. There is no rush. Come from the position that neither of you is steering the exchange to a particular conclusion or is attached to a specific outcome. Stay in the present with each other without coloring your experience with preconceptions or projections. Don't be concerned with "being right" or "who is right." This will quickly dissipate any feeling of tension and create an atmosphere that is without charge.

The issue of preconceptions and projections is a tricky one because we all have these, to some extent or another. The task is to find a way to set these aside and allow something new to be introduced. There are generally more possibilities in a situation than we initially imagine, and holding onto a position only blocks us from seeing those other possibilities. As you practice this process, you will find it becomes easier, and that you look upon your exchanges as an opportunity to create, and to be surprised with something new and fresh. You will find that you come to appreciate that your partner has different views and ideas that expand the possibilities available to you. By not freeze-framing a specific expectation or outcome, you will experience that your partner introduces a variety into life that would not otherwise be there, and you will really begin to welcome change rather than resisting it.

Trust the Process

Don't fall off the wagon! Every time you feel yourself losing contact with your partner and getting defensive or argumentative, keep in mind that you are in this together, and return to the emotional connection you committed to at the start. Even though you might not see it yet, believe a result is possible, and that the two of you want to reach it together. Reaffirm this to your partner.

If your partner slips, don't join him or her; instead, help them back by remaining committed to a shared solution. This is the point at which you can make a conscious choice to act differently. One small change will cause a different reaction, and the entire discussion can take an alternate path. By refusing to let conflict in, even if it comes from your partner, your response can change the entire tenor of the exchange.

A young girl asked her grandmother, "How did you and Grandpa stay married for so long?" Her grandmother thought about it for a long while and said, "We never fell out of love at the same time." Sometimes, one person believing in the relationship can be enough to keep it on track.

Expect the Unexpected

The results of this process are quite surprising, and you will discover a real sense of pleasure at tackling the issue together. As ideas, viewpoints and feelings are exchanged between the two of you, the results go way beyond either of your original concepts, and you will reach a place that works for both of you that neither of you imagined initially. It is not a product of compromise, but rather something your openness and acceptance of each other has created. You may have changed your position as a result of this process, but you have not been forced to give anything up.

After using this approach on a few problems, you get a feel for it. Literally. A sense of delight and intimacy arises when you find a mutual solution. Your positive experiences accumulate and bring with them assurance and peace, combined with the knowledge that acting in union you can find answers and resolutions that are far more than either of you have conceived of alone.

This style is something that can be cultivated. Seek for the positive and come from love. It feels and works so much better than manipulation, force, pressuring, anger, self-righteousness, control or separation. Most of all, it is important to remember that this is not some hard, heavy struggle. You are playing: sharing your individual selves while actively co-creating the "we." This is a dance you are doing together; make it light and make it joyful. We wish you much delight as you experience this process and the surprising transformation it brings.

Conversations with Other Couples

JAMES AND RITA

Q: How do you deal with disagreements?

RITA: I think we don't fight because neither one of us wants drama. I've had so much drama in my life. I just wanted peace and I did that consciously. I don't want fighting; I don't want upsets and all that, so we started using humor and it works really effectively for us. I think we both do it. When I feel neglected I'll go "Oh God, I'm so neglected" and dramatize it. [Rita mimes a Victorian melodrama.] I'll make fun of myself and the feelings; not that my feelings aren't real, but I go to therapy with that. Also, at the beginning, I would talk about whatever I was upset about with other people, and then come to James in a cleaner way; not blaming, but talking about my needs more than "You did this." The humor has been really helpful for me. I will dramatize and exaggerate and then we'll both laugh, but I still get to say my feelings. Saying that I'm feeling neglected and what are we going to do about it is just heavier, so I like to use humor because we're always laughing. I think I've laughed with James more than anybody.

JAMES: Yes, because it's a good way; if something's bothering you it's a good way to bring it up because then we talk about it and what to do as far as how to solve the problem. But nobody gets mad and we always seem to have a good time with it.

RITA: Another way we handle things is trying to say it in a

non-blaming way. For example, when we first met I used to make dinner all the time and he would show up late a lot, and so instead of saying that I make all this dinner and then it's cold, I tried to say it in a different way that wasn't offensive. I said that I admire you so much that I just want to please you, and that when I make dinner for you and you're late, I don't feel it's important to you, I don't feel valued. He's been on time ever since; that's eight years of being on time, when before, that wasn't the case until I communicated how important that was.

JAMES: Yes, it came down to the fact that I wasn't showing respect for her putting in all that time and effort.

RITA: James is incredible – I mean, he adapts to requests and that's pretty amazing. He's not self-righteous or mean; there's not a mean bone in his body and he's a kind person.

ANNE AND JOHN

Q: How do you deal with disagreements?

JOHN: I leave (laughing).

ANNE: I think it is actually a very good thing to sometimes leave and go sit somewhere quietly. If there are really angry responses, angry feelings that come up, my way of looking at it is that it's better to let that simmer down, let it dissipate, and wait until you're able to speak more rationally.

JOHN: Me too. I have to stop and go, "Okay John, you may be slow but you're not stupid, so go think about this for awhile."

Sometimes we struggle in our own communications, because I know what I'm thinking, and I'm trying desperately to pay attention to the words that I use, but somehow or another that doesn't seem to pass muster, and you hear something different than what I was saying. I know that I can't read your mind. I also know you can't read mine, so if I need something, I need to let you know that I need something, and if you need something you need to let me know, because when I try to read your mind, more often than not, I'm wrong; I don't have it right, because I'm still learning who you are.

ANNE: But I think we really do have a very good capacity and technique to sit down when there is a disagreement or misunderstanding, and be able to listen to each other and to put it all out on the table. I think for the most part we do that with responsible communications. What I mean by that is that I try to refrain from making angry "You" statements. I try to own it, I try to speak in terms of what my experience is and take ownership of it, and basically to be respectful of you as a person, to be loving of you, to avoid anger, condemnation, abusive language. That doesn't even come up. It's mostly about taking responsibility for one's experience. I want to be able to say everything I'm thinking and feeling. I don't want to hold it back, and I try to say that compassionately and ditto for you, John: "What do you need? What's bothering you? What is it that you want?" and just put it all out and then work it out. I can't think of a time when we were not able to work out an issue.

JACKY AND MICHAEL

Q: How do you deal with disagreements?

JACKY: When I see something I don't like, I say to myself, "Jacky, you need to tell him. Don't put it under the rug because it's going to grow there, and it's going to create a bump, and it just kind of poisons the well, sooner or later. Tell him right now!" Again, don't assume that he's going to read your mind, and he's going to change or something. You have to tell him what you don't like and negotiate. I mean relationship is a constant negotiation: "OK, I'm gonna change a little bit to the way you want, but don't assume that I'm always going to switch for you."

I don't want to change him. If there are certain things that he likes to do a certain way, go for it, but if you don't talk about it, it starts to have a negative effect on the relationship, so when there's things I don't like, I observe myself and think, "Jacky, you need to tell him." I almost feel like there's a higher self looking at me and saying "This time, it's going to be different, and you're going to have to be straight instead of stuffing it."

MICHAEL: That's one of the things I so appreciate with Jacky. She is very candid, sometimes blunt, but I'd rather take that than having a smile with a frown beneath it, and dissimulation and lack of transparency and everything – you know, the pretending that everything's OK. I will not tolerate that any more in my life, period, because it never ever works. And so yeah, sometimes when she'll tell me something, I have to stop for a moment. In the past, in previous relationships, I'd get defensive, because I took it as an attack, but Jacky never means it as an attack. She's just saying this is how she's perceiving it, and this is why it doesn't work for her. Then I'll observe myself, the ego side of myself, wanting to react to it, and then I'll just say, "Alright, you know what, she's telling me something valuable."

JACKY: Let me give a specific example. In my family where I grew up, my mom would always say "Don't ever waste food." You just put it away in the refrigerator and eat it tomorrow. Don't throw food away; it's wired in my brain from my childhood. I don't know what to do about it but listen. When I go over to Michael's on the weekends, I cook, sometimes too much, and I leave the leftovers for his meal on Monday. So one time, I came the next weekend and I saw the food was still there. The first time I didn't say anything. I just thought, oh well, he forgot it. Second time, oh well, he's too busy. Third time, I'm going to have to tell him, this is not going well. So I said, "Honey, I have to tell you something. This is how my mom brought me up. It's how I grew up in my childhood. And I have that in me not to waste food. So if you don't want the leftovers, tell me, I'll take them with me and I'll eat them." And so now we have that understanding. He will tell me, "Honey, I don't eat the food and I forget it, so it's better if you take it with you, or if you leave it, I'll make sure I eat it." And so there you go – you just talk about it, any problem, and see how you can solve these issues. It's simple, it's silly, but you have to talk about it.

MICHAEL: Well, I think what it is, you're "afraid of hurting that person's feelings," where really what you're afraid of is their reaction to what you might say, and you get abandonment issues and all kinds of things. Like this last time, I hadn't eaten any of the food she had left, and after I discovered that, I thought "Oh my God, it's been a week," so I just tossed it, and when she saw that, she said, "Honey, I've got something I have to tell you – this kind of hurt my feelings."

JACKY: I felt hurt that you just threw it away, you see; you have to talk about it.

MICHAEL: And we did, and I apologized. The point is, avoiding reactive behavior.

JACKY: Like shouting the thing out or fighting instead. That doesn't work out a problem.

MICHAEL: So as far as disagreements go, be totally authentic and transparent about your communications, and then avoid being reactive to what is being said. Those are the crucial areas.

DIANE AND MARK

Q: How do you solve problems?

MARK: One thing that I feel we're working on is how we address each other, how we argue, how we talk to each other, how we get things across – the things that are bothering us – and how to do it so the other person doesn't get hurt and so we don't escalate the intensity of the situation. We're both quite different – the way I deal with things I'm more down here and I feel that

Diane sometimes can get very loud very quickly and I'm not used to that. I grew up in a household where the emotion was really tapped down and repressed and I was used to that. If my dad raised his voice or something, or an argument started, then all of a sudden my mom would say that the neighbors were going to hear, and they would tamp it down right away. With our relationship, it seems like depending on what's going on with Diane and what's going on with me psychically, sometimes I'll say something and she'll take umbrage and the level of the voice goes up and the intensity goes up and I have to take it upon myself to defuse the situation. I think that we're learning how to fight – how to fight fairly and not get it to escalate to a point where you are actually inflicting wounds that are going to be hard to fix.

DIANE: So that's where the good will comes in.

MARK: We've accumulated good will over the years.

DIANE: I also think even when we argue, which we do, that I don't want to be stuck in that place. Rarely in 23 years have we gone to bed angry with each other. Usually there's either some resolution or an agreement that this is crazy and nobody wants to be in that place.

MARK: So it's pretty important in our relationship that we try to not let things linger.

DIANE: Or fester.

MARK: Fester, or get out of hand, so we spend a lot of time working on that. I think I'm more inclined to try to stop it, to try to put some consciousness into it; that a lot of times, I'll go "Now Diane, your voice is like 10dB up."

DIANE: That sometimes gets me even more riled up.

MARK: Yes, sometimes that antagonizes her.

DIANE: Sometimes you're talking about the effect and not about the problem and what causes the voice. It becomes about, "Oh, you're not acting right," rather than "Let's talk about what the problem is."

MARK: What I find works for me is that I lower my decibels and I try to make my voice calmer and slower, and sometimes that works. Just by lowering my voice, becoming calmer, sometimes that'll bring the whole thing down.

DIANE: Because I can see that I'm being unreasonable.

MARK: That works better than accusing her.

Q: How do you deal with disagreements?

MARK: Well, we have disagreements all the time, and usually what we do is that I'll state what I think we should do, and then she'll come back with "Yes, but..." and we'll go back and forth, and if we can't resolve it that way then sometimes we'll say "Well, gimme some time to think about it."

DIANE: Agree to disagree.

MARK: And then we'll bring it up later.

DIANE: I like to figure out how to come to a win/win: how both people can get their needs met.

MARK: That's the tricky part of the relationship.

DIANE: I am much more – I'll blurt out something; Mark's not a blurter. I sort of react and then you sort of come back more reasoned and then we go from there. But I often need to just express myself. I'm more emotionally expressive than you are. Something else that helps is not to say 'Always' or 'Never.'

MARK: Yeah, we call each other out on the 'always' stuff.

DIANE: You never do this, you always do that.

MARK: We always call each other on that one.

DIANE: That's the finger-pointing you, but taken to the next level.

MARK: For one thing it's untrue and basically it's unfair.

DIANE: Yes, and we're both conscious about not blaming.

Being Present

When you love someone, the best thing you can offer is your presence. How can you love if you are not there?
Thich Nhat Hanh

BEING PRESENT MEANS paying attention to what is actually happening. We get on so well because we practice this with each other; what is in the moment is more important to us than what has happened or what might happen. This act of presence brings magic and mystery. We are joyously involved in creating our experiences together, allowing everything to feel new, original and full of discovery. This undefended way of living and being imbues our union with peace and passion. Even though this has threaded itself throughout our relationship, we never take this for granted, but rather always celebrate it.

A Conversation

MAUDE: If I was going to point out one of the most important characteristics of our togetherness, I'd have to say it's the way we're present with each other.

PHIL: And the thing about being present is that I am drawn to it naturally. I don't know what caused it, though; I don't know that I have a ready answer for that.

MAUDE: When we first came together, we were very much paying attention to each other. Attention is a very critical part of presence, and in our case, that never went away; it didn't change. We continued paying attention to each other, staying in that place that you're often in at the beginning of a relationship. We didn't lose that quality.

PHIL: Right, good point – that first flush of interest, of attention.

MAUDE: Yeah – I always feel like I have your attention. I always feel like you're really interested, and that you see me, and many other things that make me feel really good come from this deep-seated sense.

PHIL: Yes, and I think the reason I give you that attention, and why it comes so easily, is that I get a lot from it – I get your attention, and I get the sense of being with someone else.

MAUDE: And being seen, I would have to say, is a strong part of it. I've always felt like you see me for who I am; it's part of your being with me. You're really with me – with the me that I see as me [laughs], not some construct in your mind.

PHIL: Right, and one of the things that makes all of this easy is that it's safe to be with you, not in an infantile safety sense, but safe in the sense that I am not going to be criticized or attacked, and I get the sense of being appreciated and loved. But not everyone holds onto this quality in their relationships like we have.

MAUDE: Well, I think that one is naturally present in the early meetings, coming together, because you're very there. You want to get to know this person. You're there with all of you trying to find out who it is. "Is it something for me? Are we connected?" So you start out very present, and I think people recede from that place, either because things don't resonate, you know, like core values, or distance begins to implant itself there because hurts or injuries occur, and protections begin. In our case, we never left that place; nothing that was there ever caused us to pull back, or to defend, and our core values resonated, so we went more in, not less in. There was no pull-back from that initial time of paying full attention to each other.

What Keeps Us From Being Present

Being present takes intention, and to do this we need to step out of learned patterns of behavior. There are good reasons for why we are not always present, as it is not always the most desirable state. Sometimes the future needs attention too, so you try to control the world in order to make your imagined future come to pass. As a species, our survival strategies of learning from the past and predicting the future have been hugely successful, so much so that we habitually treat most of our experience in those terms. There are times when that is appropriate, but often it's like ordering the next meal while you're still eating the current one.

Another way that we process our experiences is through language: everything is categorized and named. The very act of naming something connects it to other images and meanings we have with the word. As soon as you use a word, all your associations with that word are brought to bear. In contrast, by being present, you see all the individual and unique qualities before you.

We need to transcend our past experience, our predictive abilities, and our linguistic classifications, because all of that is static. Newness, novelty and growth arise out of the present.

To get past these mental models of the world, consider some aspects of the present:

- It is unspeakable, by definition. It cannot be captured in words. It is like a reflection in a pool; if you reach out to grasp it, the ripples of words only hide the reflection.

- It is primary. Our entire verbal and intellectual edifice is derived from our experience.

- It has a timeless quality. It's not eternal in the sense of lasting forever, but in the sense of being outside of time.

- It's constantly new. This moment has never been before.

With these aspects of the present in mind, the question becomes how we bring this into our interactions with our partner. Intention is key. Come to your partner with openness and acceptance. Put aside desires for specific outcomes. Be available with an empty mind.

Being fully present in a relationship has a transformative effect. By giving full attention to what is present, you can see your partner more clearly, and hear more clearly what they are saying. By relinquishing the need to control the future, you also by definition give up attempts to control the other person. By not being concerned with the past or the future, a huge pool of possible conflicts is defused. Almost always, dealing with the present is the way to go. When problems arise, you can't deal with them by avoidance. Mentally screaming "No, I don't want that spilt milk in my life!" doesn't help. You'll have to mop it up at some point before you can move on.

Frequently avoidance of the present leads to idealization of the future... When an event does not live up to your expectations you can get out of the depression by idealizing again. Do not let this vicious circle become your life-style. Interrupt it now with some strategic present-moment fulfillment.

Wayne W. Dyer, *Your Erroneous Zones*

Being Present with Your Partner

An impediment to being fully present is when you encounter aspects of your partner that bug you. The first step in dealing with this is with language. By speaking in the present tense, the focus remains on what is present, rather than inviting conflict about the past or the future.

Also, remember to speak from the "I," not from the "you." Say "I feel embarrassed when you complain about the service," rather than "You shouldn't talk to the waiter like that." The statement "I feel..." is personal, and is about the present, whereas "You should..." is an attempt to control the other person.

Speaking personally does several things. It removes criticism from the conversation, which reduces the chance of reflexive counter-responses from your partner, allowing space for an open and honest response instead. It is still possible that your partner will read an attack into your words, especially if they have a history of being criticized. Just calmly explain that you are only talking about how you feel.

By expressing your feelings, you create a situation where your partner has direct information about you, and may change as a result of his or her knowledge of your reactions. When you instead criticize, that information is missing, and your partner can only infer where you are at.

Lastly, speaking personally adds intimacy because you have exposed your feelings. It invites a corresponding personal response.

Next, look at your own reactions. Do they arise from force of habit: "I've always put the cutlery handles down in the dishwasher." What is the source of your irritation? Many times it is simply an assumption of how things ought to be, based on the past, and that assumption can be overcome by looking at things as they actually are — that is, by being in the present. It is possible that your reaction is from something deep-seated and meaningful to you, but if it's not a deal breaker, look hard inside yourself at your reaction and what is behind it. In the end, you can't change your partner; you can only change yourself. When you do this, it often produces a different response, to which you in turn act differently, and so on, and a chain reaction takes place that reaches a completely different conclusion.

The Power of Presence

Presence is a matter of the degree to which you are focused on and experiencing the events in front of you. Being present is responding to what is actually happening, rather than reacting according to your previous experiences, fears, or future concerns; you are neither coloring what is with occurrences from the past, nor looking for a specific future outcome.

Being present brings an experience of newness. Nothing is ever the same, and it is very mysterious and counter-intuitive. You would think that settling in for a movie or walking around the park would become drab through familiarity. However, they don't. They are intrinsically different – life is not like the movie "Groundhog Day." When you are not constrained by your past, it gives you an extraordinary sense of potential and growth. Change is not suppressed in favor of what has been, nor rejected in fear of what might happen. The result is a sense that you always have more to do and explore.

Being in presence allows you to create rather than repeat; it allows a free flow of ideas and exchanges that encourage intimacy. The present is the world we actually live in. The past and the future are merely aids we have devised to manage it; don't mistake the utensils for the meal.

Practicing presence adds great richness to your life; problems fall away, and you experience a wonderful sense of joy. The power of this practice within a relationship has no limits.

Think of the jazz improv artist responding to the musical banter among her fellow players onstage. Aside from whatever training they've done in advance, as soon as the curtain opens, they move into unknown territory together, creating something new each time by remaining in a state of undivided presence.

Donna Quesada, *The Buddha in the Classroom*

Conversations with Other Couples

JACKY AND MICHAEL

Q: Is being present important within your relationship? What role does it play?

MICHAEL: Presence is the foundation of our relationship – being heart open. If I hadn't made that shift, we wouldn't be sitting here, I doubt if we'd be together.

JACKY: I don't think the relationship exists without it.

MICHAEL: Without it, we couldn't have what we have.

JACKY: A plant can't grow without water.

MICHAEL: Or the sun. It is the sun, it is the water, it is the soil. It's all. Being fully present for us is absolutely everything.

JACKY: Maybe sometimes you have to make a statement. What I mean by that is you actually say "I'm here for you, right now." Every moment I am with him is sacred, and we really want to make it high quality, so for that we make a declaration of our presence.

JAMES AND RITA

Q: Is being present important within your relationship? What role does it play?

RITA: James is the most present person I've ever met. He's really there. I mean, just in general, he's there. So it's that closeness that I always craved. The intimacy. And just like every night he rubs my feet and we talk about the day or people or whatever. It's very intimate.

ANNE AND JOHN

Q: Is being present important within your relationship? What role does it play?

JOHN: For me its awareness. You know, of who you are and where you are and what you are doing. That, and trying to be sensitive to your being.

ANNE: To be present, to other people, in terms of just dropping yourself, and putting all of one's attention and mindfulness on the other person, and just being in that space of whatever happens between the two people.

I think that's just my nature in general, not that I practice it 100% of the time. It's very hard to do that 100% of the time, but it is my intention. Sometimes I am in a hurry, so I'm not paying good attention, but I generally have the intention, whoever I am with, to really listen and try to mentally drop (which is a Zen technique) what's on my mind – just put it aside. But because we are two people living together, I think the tendency could be to get lazy with that. I think for us and any two people living together for a long time, one has to keep renewing that commitment to really pay attention, to be new and open in the moment, rather than think "Oh, I know what he's going to say, I know what he's going to do," because then you stop really paying attention. You're not as open to what's happening with the other person; you think you know, but, you might get sloppy, you might get lazy and may not pay such high quality attention.

Sexuality, Intimacy and Union

FOR US, as for many couples, sexuality is a place where we have a direct experience of union – a sense that we have merged to form one body. The sense of self as an individual, separate experience still remains, but there is this additional sense of connectedness. Sex is like a step-ladder; it enables us to reach a higher place, a vista of union that transcends the physical.

These are times of deep intimacy when we come so close to each other that we merge – literally. An additional sense of the two of us – a joint body – is palpable.

It's not the sense of self, and it's not the sense of the other; it's a distinct fusion of the two. It usually arises during sex, but we also experience it at other times of intimacy. The path to it involves being completely present and also undefended, and this leads to a shared consciousness, a way of being that is neither of us individually.

The directness of this experience trumps all theories and verbal discussions. We have found that this knowledge of what union is becomes a part of the fabric of how we are with each other all the time.

The Gateway of Sex

So what is necessary to reach this kind of union with your partner? It requires dropping boundaries and relating from an undefended state. Sex offers a gateway to this experience. Your normal ego state is like a room that you live in. Sexual union opens a door in that room to another state, that of a shared self. To leave the room and enter that shared space, you have to let go of the idea that your separate self is all that there is. You continue to have the experience of self, but another experience is simultaneously available – the united self.

It is important to believe that this is possible; if you don't, you are less likely to see it when it is happening, and less likely to acknowledge the event afterward. If you don't enter this state, you remain two separate people, each having their own experience. This can be wonderful, as we all know, but sex also offers the additional opportunity of union.

This opportunity to experience union in a non-verbal way allows you to move into this state through the actual knowledge of what union is and of what it feels like. This kind of knowledge only comes from direct experience. Once you have consciously recognized the experience, you can open to it, allow it, and foster it within your relationship. Sex can offer the kind of direct experience of merging that transcends the questions that arise from the paradox of being an individual and at the same time being a part of a united being.

Mutuality

There are a number of characteristics afforded by sexual union that are of note. One of the most startling is the indisputable mutuality of what is experienced. The merged self, and the experiences thereof, are shared and are clearly the same. There is a quality of complete agreement that confounds the mind, and yet it is undeniably there in the shared experience.

A Conversation

MAUDE: In this area of the mutuality of experience that we talk about and try to find words for, there are two elements that are startling and at the same time critical to describing this state. One is that we're both very clear that we're having the same experience.

PHIL: Yes, right.

MAUDE: It's very very certain through many experiences that we completely and totally agree in every way.

When we try to bring it into words and describe what's happening to each other, it's totally the same. We clearly are having the same exact experience – and we're very convinced of that, very firm on that, there's no "Well, wait a minute," or "It's a little bit different for me."

PHIL: We've confirmed this again and again by talking about the experience and having the other person say "Yes, yes, yes," and agreeing completely with how it is, difficult though it is to talk about the experience, because it so rapidly goes beyond words –

MAUDE: Exactly.

PHIL: – and it's such an experiential thing that it's very difficult to speak about it, but to the extent that we can speak about it, you agree with my words and vice versa.

MAUDE: Yes. The other element that I feel is a critical component is this sense of two separate selves which remain totally and completely uniquely individual – you're you and I'm me and there's no impingement on that – nothing. I haven't given anything up, I'm retaining my total separate self, but at the same time there's this very strong experience of a merged self, and it's in that merged self that we have the same thoughts, because there's one mind in that merged self, that place of union. Do you know what I mean?

PHIL: Yes, exactly. My comments would be kind of intellectual. As a rational thinking person, I always struggle with this because it is so different from my usual experience of the world. I have no place to put it, and so when I am away from it, it's very hard for me to think about it and talk about it because I don't know what to say about it in other terms. I don't know how to connect it – how to explain it. It's a different framework, but the experience of it at the time is undeniable.

MAUDE: Absolutely.

PHIL: It's experiential. It is there, and one of the things about it is the sense that it's not directly sexual at all, that the sexuality is only a gateway, a key, a step-ladder, a way of gaining entrance to this mutual place. And the union is not physical. It is enabled by the physicality but it is not the physicality; that to me is very clear.

MAUDE: Yes, exactly.

The Paradox of Union

This experience of union that we have described has no place in the Western materialist view of the world which sees our individual bodies operating largely autonomously, with consciousness arising in some unknown way from the complexity of the brain. Many studies are finding that the decisions we make are influenced by factors outside our conscious awareness, casting ever more doubt on the validity of our perceptions.

It was not always so. Early philosophers such as Descartes and Berkeley took our senses to be primary, and doubted what we could know about the world. Berkeley even denied its independent existence. Since then, the scientific method has transformed our understanding of the world. Its approach is to make observations, develop a hypothesis that explains them, then make predictions from that hypothesis and see if they are true. Upon validation, the hypothesis is elevated to the status of a theory. This approach has been so spectacularly successful that objective truth is now primary, and, among the scientific community, "subjective" is now a pejorative term.

Yet there are a number of arguments, both from reason and experience, that support an alternative view.

Firstly, we are positioned within a hierarchy. An atom is part of a molecule is part of a cell is part of an organ is part of a human body is part of a species is part of life is part of the planet, etc. Any of these is what Arthur Koestler called a holon: something that is complete in itself, yet part of a larger whole.

Although we like to think of ourselves as independent beings, we are actually all vitally interrelated. Human beings are incredibly social creatures. We need to interact with other human beings to keep ourselves sane. Even apart from our social needs, the reality is that very few of us can survive alone. Go off and live for a year in the wilderness if you disagree. Don't take anything you didn't make from scratch. No Bowie knife unless you smelted the steel yourself. The products of civilization such as freeways, houses and jetliners are all produced by the cooperative skills of many people. Just as different cells make up an animal body, so do these groups of people make up the body of society.

Our identification with the self is so strong that we tend to overlook our identification with these larger groups. When asked to describe yourself, you might say, among other things, that you are a Texan, a plumber, an

American, a Mets fan, a poker player. Sometimes these identifications are so strong that they transcend the pull for personal survival. For example, the mother who would die for her child, the soldier who would die for his country, or the suicide bomber who would die for a cause.

There are other times when the sense of self weakens. Sometimes, when alone in nature, we can have the sense of being part of a larger whole.

Gurus and wise men throughout the ages have spoken of the unity found through transcendence of the self, and people to this day continue to report this. Are we to take them all as mad? Deluded? People also report transcendence through the use of hallucinogens. The very name disparages the experience.

When sex is approached, not as a solitary experience of intense stimulation, but as a way of being with another person, then a merging is possible. When full openness removes all barriers, the boundaries between two people can dissolve.

Union in Everyday Life

When you are fortunate enough to have a direct knowledge of union through sex, it gives you a foundation upon which to build this characteristic into your day-to-day relationship. You have learned that it is possible to remain an intact, whole self and be in merged union with another at the same time. Much of the conflict that couples experience comes from the belief that there are different sides, and the resulting feeling of having to defend one's side against attack and invasion.

We are so used to going about our lives as individuals that it can be hard to see the element of union in shared activities, and it therefore requires fostering and a degree of attention to do so. Look for the feeling of operating as a unit, an item, a pair. The satisfaction when you and your partner successfully carry a piece of furniture upstairs contains this joint experience; look for the "We did it" feeling, rather than the "You and I did it" feeling. Foster it within your relationship. When you come from this viewpoint, it reduces the feeling of being on different sides, of being right, of being in opposition to your partner, and everything else that can arise from seeing yourself as a separate disconnected individual.

The more this shared experience occurs, the more it will permeate and illuminate your day-to-day relationship. Every time you experience union, be it through sexual means or any other avenue, your ability to live in peace and love is greatly enhanced.

Conversations with Other Couples

JAMES AND RITA

Q: Is sex important within your relationship? What role does it play?

JAMES: Yes, it's been important. We're really affectionate but it doesn't always have to be sex. Right now in our current situation with Rita's injury, it's been a long time, so sex hasn't actually happened for a while, but we're always affectionate and close and every night we just snuggle up and talk and spend time together and so that's just as good.

RITA: James rubs my feet every night and we're constantly touching all day long.

JAMES: Yeah, that's one thing I've always missed – a real close physical relationship, and we have that here.

RITA: I think the glue that holds us together is the touch and the affection. We are always touching; it's what I've always wanted.

JAMES: Actually both of us always wanted that type of a close affectionate relationship.

RITA: In the beginning before we had sex I would say to him, "Tell me something personal," and I did that from the very beginning. Our talks started to become deeply personal, and I think that's why we still love going to bed early and cuddling and talking. It was just opening up more and more and so sex was the carrot, you remember that?

JAMES: Yes, we'd have this romantic evening and everything, and get in bed and then it's like, "So tell me something personal," and oh my God, I would sit there and it would take me a while to come up with something to talk about. But then once I got going and really started sharing, we wound up with a really close relationship, and it was really smart that she did that.

DIANE AND MARK

Q: Is sex important within your relationship? What role does it play?

DIANE: I would say that a physical relationship is an area that is also important and that's something that ebbs and flows, but we love each other in that way, and there's passion and there's juiciness. There's appreciation for each other as physical selves and this is also sustaining in the relationship.

MARK: It is important, and what's important is that every once in a while it's really good to have some intimate time, because it just resets everything. It just puts everything in a whole different perspective. Everything falls back and you're back in Eden again and then you get a fresh start, and we both feel the same way. The thing that bothers me is that I just wish that we were more intimate more often, but I don't want to push the subject. I want it to be natural; I want to feel it. I want both of us to feel it, and I think that what happens is when we both feel it at the same time it's more of a natural thing. Instead of saying "Why don't we have some play time?" I've come to realize that it's gonna happen at some point — it's the timing, it has to

be just right. And you can't really push it, you can't ca-
jole. I think we've finally just got into some kind of a
rhythm.

DIANE: Yeah, I think there's a recognition on both our
parts that the other person is passionate sexually. It's
an area in which we've had a very close connection
from the get-go, and it only gets better. It may not be
as frequent, but it gets deeper and more cosmic.

MARK: It's not the frequency that's important.

DIANE: It's the depth, the depth of feeling and the intensity of the feeling. Appreciation of the other person as
a lover.

MARK: But it is important, a very important part.

DIANE: I think we both enjoy our intimate times. There
are ways to be intimate without having sex, too, that's
the other thing – more touching and cuddling, laying
on the couch together and watching TV – there's intimacy in all of that.

MARK: Or even just cuddling at night, you know, once in a
while, or touching. Sometimes I notice that in the middle of the night she's kind of moaning and talking in
her sleep and sometimes I'll put my hand on her back
and just touch her, and she'll relax and just go back to
sleep so… stuff like that. We try to acknowledge each
other and bring that intimacy into our everyday life.
We're so busy going back and forth, that sometimes
we just stop each other and say "Let's have a hug" or
something like that, and I think we're getting better at
doing that kind of thing more often.

DIANE: Yes, hug breaks are great.

JACKY AND MICHAEL

Q: Is sex important within your relationship? What role does it play?

MICHAEL: We make a distinction between sex and physical intimacy. We see sex as an act, and intimacy as a connection. Intimacy can happen between two people at the physical, emotional and spiritual level. So, the word 'sex' is kind of a charged word. I am not capable – physically capable – of intercourse and that's what most people consider sex. Now physical intimacy? Absolutely. That is crucial to our relationship; it's part of how we express ourselves. This right here [Jacky and Michael are holding hands and sitting close together] is physical intimacy; it's not sex, but it's physical intimacy, which frankly I find far more fulfilling than intercourse. And yes, there are times when our physical intimacy edges into the phase of genital stimulation, orgasm and all that, and that's wonderful, it's beautiful, and it exceeds what most people consider to be humanly possible.

JACKY: Sometimes just breathing, and we sit in front of each other and we breath.

MICHAEL: Yeah, we breathe and we get that cycle of energy going, and then we're into the realm of spiritual intimacy – like when we were kissing on the beach on your birthday, and then we collapsed into unity, and it was like "Did you just feel what I felt? Wow!"

JACKY: It is important. I would never want he and I to be like room-mates. I want us to always feel fresh. When I touch him, when we kiss – we kiss a lot – we look at each other eye-to-eye, and smell – ooh, the sense of smell! I love his smell, and I say that frequently. It's so yummy. It's important. You have to just express what you feel, and not be afraid to say it. It's fertilizer for our relationship.

MICHAEL: We are both very uninhibited, sexually speaking, and in the past, that was always a problem with my previous relationships because I tended to be far more uninhibited than my partner would be at that time. With Jacky, that's not a problem at all, and it's wonderful because we are constantly exploring new facets of all forms of intimacy. Like afterward, we're going "What was that? Holy Cow!" and it's all intuitive, and its just spontaneous.

Peace

Peace is a conscious choice.
John Denver

O NE OF THE MOST SURPRISING aspects of our relationship is the direct experience of peace that it engenders. This follows naturally from the alternatives to conflict that we practice. For us, peace is not a void described by the absence of conflict, anger or war. Peace is an actual experience. It is filled with calm, assurance of goodness, acute awareness of presence, acceptance of what is, joy, and overflowing love. It is both intense passionate happiness and quiet, rock-solid reassurance. Peace permeates all of our interactions and is our underpinning, our foundation. We are convinced that this knowledge and the direct experience of actual peace can be available in every relationship.

Peace Through Acceptance

One of the keys to knowing true peace within your relationship is practicing acceptance. This occurs when neither of you participates in the one-upmanship of power struggles or the insistence on being right. When you truly accept your partner, you are not busy trying to make them someone else.

Practicing this kind of acceptance eliminates the root of much of the conflict and alienation people have in their relationships. Instead, it leads to a state of peace that cannot really be imagined before experiencing it. The kind of calm and relaxation that emerges when you do not feel the need to defend or protect your person is filled with joy and creative power.

There should be no higher calling for you than to meet your partner's need for acceptance. If you want peace and tranquility, you must approach the task of managing your intimate relationship with a general spirit of acceptance.
Phil McGraw, *Relationship Rescue*

Peace Through Individuality

The same is true when you truly honor the individuality of your partner. It is surprising and very revealing to see how much of a challenge it can be to recognize that, no matter how much you and your partner share core values, you are still distinctly different and completely unique individuals. When you treat your partner's views and feelings as having as much validity as your own, you offer a place where they can exist in comfort: they do not have to bend down because the ceiling is too low; they need not avoid the side of the couch where the springs stick out; they don't need to step outside to stretch. There is no need to find a more comfortable abode.

It requires a secure sense of your own individuality to take the leap of accepting your partner as a separate individual, and to understand that this strengthens your union and doesn't challenge it. When you not only recognize this, but also value and rejoice in this separateness and difference, you are creating that free and undefended state in both yourself and your partner that is so necessary for peace to exist.

Peace Through Our Process

Acceptance and the recognition and celebration of your partner's individuality creates an atmosphere in which you can apply the process we have talked about. Using this process for resolving differences and making decisions is a very positive experience, and consequently there is no reticence to having these problem-solving sessions, nor do you accumulate negativity that barbs your relationship. On the contrary, the fruits of such discussions are very enjoyable. They generate a positive experience of a shared creative act which contains the dual experience of having reached a resolution, while at the same time connecting very deeply with each other.

The more you use this process and the more knowledge you have of its creative outcomes, the more you will come to trust in its availability, and the more your relationship will become a serene zone of peace.

Peace Through Presence

Our dissatisfactions rarely arise from what is in front of us. Instead, our past learning and our future fears intrude to disturb our peace. Our knowledge of the world takes two forms: ideas in the mind, and what we know from direct experience. Being present is a way to see that these intrusions do not exist in the world, but only in our mind. When we can see the world for how it is, we can act accordingly.

When you take this approach, you are not plagued by worries and creations of the mind. You do not see your partner in terms of the past, and you are not projecting about how they might behave; consequently, you are in an undefended state and have the opportunity to share experiences in the moment, and through these experiences, a mutual reality.

When you and your partner are truly present with each other, you both feel heard and seen. You share yourselves intimately and appreciate the other. Out of this arises a feeling of connectedness that gives you a deep-seated experience of peacefulness, relaxation and joy which can permeate your whole day.

A Conversation

MAUDE: Peace is an element I would emphasize in terms

of our relationship. I think it's at the very foundation and core of what's important to us, and comes as a result of how we are together.

PHIL: Yes. You described peace as a core value, and my initial thought was "That's weird," but I immediately realized that's true, because what is a core value if not something that I value, and I certainly value peace.

MAUDE: Yes, and we have, as I am fond of pointing out, a very passionate, peaceful relationship. It's important to me that both these elements, passion and peace, are seen together, because I know people very often associate the idea of peace with an even-keeled, maybe even slightly boring, very one-tone existence, and that's not what our experience is at all. The experience of actually living together in peace the way we do, I get shivers when I start to think about it! It is so ecstatic, so full of joy, of real joy, like freedom, total lack of stress, relaxation, a feeling of goodness that I take with me all the time. It's a really amazing thing to have the experience of peace as we do.

PHIL: If you regard the experience of peace in our relationship as a lack of conflict, where neither of us need to put any effort into resolving how we work together, such as who's doing the groceries or any of that whole list of large and small activities, that removes a whole range of distractions and allows us to experience the joys of life.

MAUDE: It also comes with the knowledge that you're not going to be attacked by your partner – I'm never expecting anything to come at me from you unawares. I'm not carrying around fortresses and defenses ever, and I have no weight on me in terms of being in your presence. I know that anything coming from you is not just accepting, but it's also really acknowledging and supportive and loving and wonderful. You're never arguing just for the sake of it, you're never wanting to push your power on me in any way, there are no power plays going on between us.

PHIL: Yes, in many ways, peace is a not doing – a process of not interfering with each other. It's an absence of power struggles, an absence of either of us pushing to be right; instead, we use our process to find only mutual solutions and decisions.

Your Goals May Reach Further Than You Think

You think you are working on yourself and your relationship, and indeed you are. But there is another unexpected component that arises from this work. Practicing peace in your relationship has results that affect more than just the two of you. Firstly, it influences other people by example. Secondly, you start treating others the same way. It ripples out into the world and, by showing what is possible, inspires people to be their best. The direct experience of peace, and the calm yet ecstatic sense of joy and love that arise from this state, is catching and very powerful. Let's go forth and change the world!

Conclusion

IT HAS BEEN a great pleasure sharing our relationship with you. We have the strong hope and desire that more of you will be able to experience the kind of ongoing peace and profound ease that we do. We have discussed how peaceful and fulfilling we find our relationship, the components that create this state, and what to look for and do so that you too can live harmoniously.

The biggest challenge is to believe that this is possible. The theme of inevitable conflict is so deeply woven into our culture, that even those teaching a non-violent approach believe that conflict must be there (because we are all different), and that the solution is to use language in a gentler way to create peace.

Let us be clear: the truth we are living is quite different. We assert again, very strongly, that inevitable conflict is a myth. Difference does not inherently cause conflict; difference can be a source of variety and joy, a gift that is a cause for celebration. Putting your attention on your commonality rather than your differences can strengthen your sense of connection and remind you that you're both on the same side.

We are convinced that the world can be transformed by radically changing each and every relationship. Intention is a key and true peace is a result. We hope we have inspired some of you to partake in this experiment of living love. Join us in spreading peace, one relationship at a time.

About the Authors

Maude and Phil Mayes live in Santa Barbara, California, having started in New York City and London, England respectively. They have been writing and speaking about spreading peace one relationship at a time for many years. They wrote the book *Secrets of a Successful Relationship Revealed,* and write a weekly relationship newsletter, as well as a weekly blog available on their website http://PhilandMaude.com. Phil and Maude are the producers of a number of relationship videos, as well as the series *Kit and Kat Relationship Experts*, all of which are to be found on their YouTube channel *The Couples Project.* They have been featured in a number of live interviews and write articles, both online and in print.

Made in the USA
Charleston, SC
03 May 2016